THE BANANA COOKBOOK

50 SIMPLE AND DELICIOUS RECIPES

SAM BROOKS

Andrews McMeel
PUBLISHING®

Andrews McMeel Publishing
a division of Andrews McMeel Universal
1130 Walnut Street, Kansas City, Missouri 64106

www.andrewsmcmeel.com

20 21 22 23 24 SHO 10 9 8 7 6 5 4 3 2 1

ISBN: 978-1-5248-6063-9
Library of Congress Control Number: 2020931390

ATTENTION: SCHOOLS AND BUSINESSES

Andrews McMeel books are available at quantity discounts with bulk purchase for educational, business, or sales promotional use. For information, please e-mail the Andrews McMeel Publishing Special Sales Department: specialsales@amuniversal.com.

CONTENTS

INTRODUCTION

There's more to the banana than meets the eye. They're well known for being delicious snacks to enjoy on their own, and they are full of energy to fuel us through the day, and potassium for a healthy heart.

But did you know that they're also great team players? Their unique nutritional makeup means they can be used in recipes as a substitute for fats, such as butter. They can also take the place of eggs and sugar in snacks, desserts, and smoothies, and they add moisture and texture to breads and cakes. Most of all, they impart that distinctive, sweet banana flavor that complements so many other foods and makes your dishes delicious.

This handy book brings you a selection of the best banana recipes, both traditional and new. Whether you like to eat your bananas hot or cold, whether you're looking for drinks, breakfast foods, tasty snacks, or a show-stopping dessert, within these pages are a range of simple recipes to inspire you, satisfy you, and celebrate this humble yellow fruit.

Welcome to *The Banana Cookbook*!

KITCHEN ESSENTIALS

Before you start baking, it's useful to know what equipment you'll need. The list below is a good indicator of what is required for most of the recipes in this book.

 Parchment paper – This is essential for lining pans and baking sheets to make sure your cakes don't stick.

 Baking sheets/pans – The ones you will need for this book are a deep 8-inch square sheet, an 8-inch square pan, an 8-inch round springform pan, a 12-cup muffin pan, a 6 by 3.5 by 3.5-inch loaf pan, an 8-inch ovenproof dish, and four 4-inch tart pans. A large, flat 11 by 8-inch baking sheet may also be useful (for toasting almonds and oats, for instance).

 Blender – This is a key piece of equipment for making smoothies.

 Cooling rack – This will ensure that your cakes, loafs, and tarts can cool down with air circulating around them and will help you to avoid soggy bottoms!

 Electric mixer or standing mixer – This helps to speed up the mixing of ingredients, although in most cases you can do it by hand, too.

 Food processor – This is a frequently used piece of equipment in this book, as it's used for blending nuts and fruit.

Measuring spoons – These allow you to accurately measure small quantities of ingredients, such as baking powder, spices, vinegar, and oils.

 Mixing bowls – At least one large mixing bowl is needed for the recipes in this book, and you may find it useful to have a few in other sizes, too.

 Muffin and cupcake liners – You will need a supply of muffin and cupcake liners for a few of the recipes in this book.

 Piping bags – You can buy reusable piping bags online or from supermarkets, or make your own from parchment paper.

 Reusable popsicle mold – For our ice pops recipe (p. 97), we recommend a reusable set of popsicle molds that come with lids/sticks. These can be purchased online or at supermarkets.

 Rolling pin – This will be useful for rolling out pastry, but if you don't have one, an empty wine bottle will work as a substitute.

 Scale – Weighing your ingredients will help your baking be as accurate as possible. However, if you prefer to use cups, use the conversion chart on the next page.

 Sieve – This is a baking essential for sifting dry ingredients. However, if you don't have one, stir dry ingredients (a bowl of flour, salt, and baking powder, for instance) with a whisk to get air into the mixture.

CONVERSIONS AND MEASUREMENTS

All the conversions in the tables below are close approximates, which have been rounded up or down. When using a recipe, always stick to one unit of measurement and do not alternate between them.

Liquid measurements

1 teaspoon = 6 milliliters

1 tablespoon
  = 15 milliliters

⅛ cup = 30 milliliters

¼ cup = 60 milliliters

½ cup = 120 milliliters

1 cup = 240 milliliters

2 tablespoons
  liquid egg white
  = 1 large egg white

Butter measurements

⅛ cup = 30 grams

¼ cup = 55 grams

⅓ cup = 75 grams

½ cup = 115 grams

⅔ cup = 150 grams

¾ cup = 170 grams

1 cup = 225 grams

Dried ingredient measurements

1 teaspoon = 5 grams

1 tablespoon = 5 grams

1 cup = 150 grams flour

1 cup = 225 grams
  superfine sugar

1 cup = 115 grams
  confectioners' sugar

1 cup = 175 grams
  brown sugar

1 cup = 200 grams
  sprinkles

DIETARY REQUIREMENTS

Many of the recipes in this book are suitable for those on a vegan or gluten-free diet. These recipes are indicated with the icons below:

 Vegan

 Gluten free

All instances of non-dairy milk, yogurt, and chocolate that are given in this book can also be switched to dairy equivalents.

BREAKFAST BITES AND MORNING PICK-ME-UPS

- Coconut, Date, and Banana Energy Balls
- Fluffy Banana and Walnut Pancakes
- Berry Smoothie Bowl with Cashews and Banana
- Chocolate and Banana Smoothie Bowl
- Nutty Banana Muesli
- Banana and Berry Oatmeal
- Creamy Almond Toast with Banana Pennies
- Nutty Banana Balls
- Date and Walnut Energy Bars
- Chocolate and Banana French Toast
- Banana-Chocolate Bites
- Banana Chips

COCONUT, DATE, AND BANANA ENERGY BALLS

These delicious energy balls are the perfect snack for when you're out and about, or they make a great, quick breakfast if prepared in advance.

METHOD

If they're not already soft, soak the dates in lukewarm water for 30 minutes, then drain.

In a food processer, blend the cashews, then add the oats and blend again to combine. Add the banana, drained dates, salt, and vanilla extract, and blend until the mixture comes together. It should be pliant enough to roll into balls.

Take the mixture, 1 heaping teaspoon at a time, and roll it into balls. If it's too sticky, put the mixture back into the food processor and add more oats. If it's too dry, add a drop of water and blend.

Roll the energy balls in the shredded coconut to finish. Keep refrigerated for up to 1 week.

MAKES

approximately 15 balls

INGREDIENTS

8 soft pitted dates
½ cup cashews
⅔ cup rolled oats
1 medium, overripe banana
Pinch of salt
½ teaspoon vanilla extract
1 cup shredded coconut

FLUFFY BANANA AND WALNUT PANCAKES

Pancakes were made for long mornings and lazy Sundays. This simple recipe makes it easier than ever to enjoy your favorite breakfast treat.

METHOD

With a fork, mash the bananas in a bowl until smooth. Add the eggs and whisk until fully incorporated.

Add in the flour and whisk again until combined.

Stir in the walnuts, nutmeg, cinnamon, and salt.

Heat the butter in a pan over medium heat. Once it is hot, pour 2 to 3 tablespoons of batter into the pan and let it cook for 30 seconds to 1 minute. Then, using a turner, flip it over and cook the other side for another 30 seconds, or until the pancake is golden brown.

Transfer onto a plate and set aside in a warm oven while you cook the other pancakes.

Serve the pancakes in a stack, and top with chopped walnuts, banana slices, and syrup.

MAKES

approximately
   6 pancakes

INGREDIENTS

2 large, overripe bananas

2 eggs

$\frac{1}{3}$ cup self-rising flour

3 tablespoons finely chopped walnuts

Pinch of ground nutmeg

$\frac{1}{2}$ teaspoon ground cinnamon

Pinch of salt

1 tablespoon butter

Chopped walnuts

Handful of ripe banana slices

Syrup of choice

BERRY SMOOTHIE BOWL WITH CASHEWS AND BANANA

This colorful dish is like eating dessert for breakfast, only it's healthy and packed with fruit!

METHOD

Add the banana, raspberries, blackberries, and yogurt to a blender and blend until smooth. If you would like a thinner consistency, add a splash of almond milk and mix again.

Pour the smoothie into a bowl and top with cashews, banana slices, and chia seeds.

SERVES

1

INGREDIENTS

1 large, ripe banana, frozen

½ cup frozen raspberries

½ cup frozen blackberries

3 heaping tablespoons non-dairy plain yogurt

Splash of almond milk (optional)

3 tablespoons cashews

½ ripe banana, sliced

1 tablespoon chia seeds

CHOCOLATE AND BANANA SMOOTHIE BOWL

This decadent breakfast smoothie bowl is the perfect way to welcome the day.

METHOD

Put the bananas, cocoa powder, yogurt, milk, and vanilla into a blender, and blend until smooth.

Pour the smoothie into a bowl, and top with the banana slices, almonds, macadamia nuts, coconut, chocolate chips, and chia seeds.

SERVES

1

INGREDIENTS

2 large, overripe bananas, frozen

2 tablespoons cocoa powder

3 tablespoons dairy-free plain yogurt

$\frac{1}{3}$ cup almond milk

$\frac{1}{4}$ teaspoon vanilla extract

$\frac{1}{2}$ ripe banana, sliced

2 tablespoons almonds

2 tablespoons macadamia nuts

1 tablespoon shredded coconut

1 teaspoon dairy-free chocolate chips

1 teaspoon chia seeds

NUTTY BANANA MUESLI

This simple recipe is a nutritional powerhouse bursting with protein and fiber to keep you feeling full until lunchtime.

METHOD

Heat oven to 350°F. Spread out the almonds (reserving 1 tablespoon) and oats on a baking sheet, and toast them in the oven for 8 to 10 minutes.

Put the oats and almonds in a bowl and mix with the walnuts, cranberries, sunflower seeds, and 2 tablespoons of the puffed rice. Stir briefly to combine.

To assemble, layer the yogurt and oat mixture in a bowl or glass. Top with banana slices and the remaining chopped almonds and puffed rice.

SERVES

1

INGREDIENTS

3 tablespoons chopped almonds, divided

⅓ cup rolled oats

3 to 4 walnuts, finely chopped

2 tablespoons dried cranberries

1 tablespoon sunflower seeds

3 tablespoons puffed rice, divided

⅓ cup non-dairy plain yogurt

½ ripe banana, sliced

BANANA AND BERRY OATMEAL

This breakfast is quick, easy, and comforting—perfect for kicking off cold winter mornings.

METHOD

Mash the banana in a bowl with a fork.

Add the banana to a small saucepan along with the oats, milk, and salt.

Heat on medium heat, stirring occasionally, until the mixture thickens and starts to bubble.

Transfer to a bowl and top with the banana slices, almonds, blueberries, and coconut.

SERVES

1

INGREDIENTS

1 overripe banana
½ cup rolled oats
1 cup non-dairy milk
Pinch of salt
½ ripe banana, sliced
2 tablespoons almonds
2 tablespoons blueberries
1 teaspoon shredded
   coconut

CREAMY ALMOND TOAST WITH BANANA PENNIES

Simple and sweet is the name of the game with this delicious breakfast idea.

METHOD

Place the bread in the toaster or in a toaster oven. While it's toasting, slice the banana.

Once the toast is done, spread each slice with a layer of cream cheese.

Top with the banana slices, honey, and almonds.

INGREDIENTS

- 2 slices whole wheat bread
- 2 tablespoons cream cheese
- 1 large, ripe banana, sliced
- 2 tablespoons honey
- 3 tablespoons almonds, broken into pieces

NUTTY BANANA BALLS

Enjoy almonds, cashews, and peanuts in these tasty, nutty bites, which are packed with protein.

METHOD

If they're not already soft, soak the dates in lukewarm water for 30 minutes, then drain.

In a food processer, blend the cashews and walnuts. Then add the almond meal, banana, salt, peanut butter, and dates, and blend until the mixture comes together. It should be pliant enough to roll into balls.

Take the mixture, 1 heaping teaspoon at a time, and roll it into balls. If it's too sticky, put the mixture back in the food processor and add more almond meal. If it's too dry, add a drop of water and blend.

Coat the energy balls in the granola to finish. To store, keep refrigerated for up to 1 week.

MAKES

approximately
15 energy balls

INGREDIENTS

8 soft pitted dates
½ cup cashews
2 tablespoons walnuts
⅔ cup almond meal
1 small, overripe banana
Pinch of salt
1 heaping teaspoon
peanut butter
⅓ cup granola (p. 61)

DATE AND WALNUT ENERGY BARS

These are the ideal grab-and-go breakfast, with no cooking required!

METHOD

Line an 8-inch square baking sheet with parchment paper. If they're not already soft, soak the the dates in lukewarm water for 30 minutes, then drain.

Place the walnuts and almonds in a food processor and blend until chopped into tiny pieces. Then add the remaining ingredients and blend until the mixture is paste-like and mixed well.

If the mixture is not coming together, add water, ½ tablespoon at a time, until it does.

Transfer the mixture to the prepared sheet, and press it down into a compact layer using the back of a spoon. Refrigerate for 3 hours, or overnight, then cut into pieces as desired.

Store in an airtight container in a cool, dry place for up to 3 weeks.

MAKES

12 to 16 bars

INGREDIENTS

10.5 ounces soft
   pitted dates
1½ cups walnuts
⅓ cup almonds
1 large, overripe banana
2 tablespoons
   cocoa powder
½ teaspoon ground
   nutmeg
Pinch of salt
1 tablespoon
   vanilla extract

CHOCOLATE AND BANANA FRENCH TOAST

Enjoy your continental breakfast with extra banana and chocolate!

METHOD

Whisk the eggs, milk, cinnamon, vanilla, and salt in a large bowl until fully incorporated.

Take two slices of bread and make a sandwich, with a third of the banana slices and chocolate pieces as filling. Dip the sandwich in the egg mixture, making sure both sides are well soaked.

Melt the butter in a frying pan over medium heat. Add the sandwich to the pan and fry for a couple of minutes on each side, or until it is golden brown and the chocolate has begun to melt. Repeat for the other two sandwiches.

Serve immediately.

INGREDIENTS

2 eggs

$\frac{2}{3}$ cup milk

$\frac{1}{2}$ teaspoon ground cinnamon

$\frac{1}{2}$ teaspoon vanilla extract

Pinch of salt

6 thick slices white bread

2 medium, ripe bananas, sliced

$4\frac{1}{4}$ ounces dark or milk chocolate, chopped

Pat of butter

BANANA-CHOCOLATE BITES

These energy balls are rich, gooey, chocolatey—and healthy!

METHOD

If they're not already soft, soak the dates in lukewarm water for 30 minutes, then drain.

In a food processer, blend the cashews. Then add the oats, banana, dates, salt, vanilla extract, and cocoa powder, and blend until the mixture comes together. It should be pliant enough to roll into balls. Then stir in the chocolate chips by hand.

Take the mixture, 1 heaping teaspoon at a time, and roll it into balls. If it's too sticky, put the mixture back in the food processor and add more oats. If it's too dry, add a drop of water and blend.

Roll the energy balls in the shredded coconut to finish. Keep refrigerated for up to 1 week.

MAKES

approximately 15 energy balls

INGREDIENTS

10 soft pitted dates

½ cup cashews

½ cup rolled oats

1 small, overripe banana

Pinch of salt

1 teaspoon vanilla extract

1 tablespoon cocoa powder

2 tablespoons dairy-free chocolate chips

⅓ cup shredded coconut

BANANA CHIPS

Enjoy these chips on their own, or add them to other dishes, such as muesli, for extra crunch and flavor.

METHOD

Preheat the oven to 225°F.

Slice the banana thinly—aim for slices no thicker than ¼ inch. Place them in a bowl with the lemon juice and mix until the slices are coated.

Line a large baking sheet with parchment paper and add the banana slices. They should be spread out and not touching each other.

Bake for 1 hour, then turn the slices over and bake for another hour. The chips should be golden around the edges, but they will not be crisp at this stage.

Once done, remove from the oven and let them cool. They should crisp up as they cool.

Eat on the same day, or store in an airtight container in a cool, dry place for up to 3 weeks.

SERVES

2

INGREDIENTS

2 large, ripe bananas
Juice of 1 lemon

CUPCAKES AND MUFFINS

- Banana and Chocolate Chip Muffins
- Vegan Chocolate Cupcakes
- Matcha and Banana Cupcakes
  with Caramelized Peanuts
- Oaty Banana Muffins
- Banana Buttercream Frosting
- Gooey Chocolate Brownies

BANANA AND CHOCOLATE CHIP MUFFINS

The combination of chocolate and banana is hard to beat—here's a recipe for the tried-and-tested favorite that's sure to go down a treat.

METHOD

Preheat the oven to 350°F and line a 12-cup muffin pan with liners.

In a large bowl, mash the bananas with a fork until fairly smooth. Then add in the sugars, egg, and melted butter, and whisk until combined.

Using a sieve, sift the flour, baking powder, baking soda, and salt into the bowl and stir with a wooden spoon to combine.

Fold in the chocolate chips and orange zest, and mix well.

Divide the mixture between the muffin liners and top with the banana slices (1 to 2 per muffin).

Bake for 15 minutes, or until the muffins are golden on the top and a toothpick comes out clean.

Let cool before serving. Store in an airtight container for up to 1 week.

MAKES

10 muffins

INGREDIENTS

2 large, overripe bananas
½ cup superfine sugar
¼ cup light brown sugar
1 egg
¼ cup butter, melted
1¾ cups self-rising flour
½ teaspoon baking powder
1 teaspoon baking soda
½ teaspoon salt
⅓ cup chocolate chips
Zest of 1 orange
12 to 20 banana slices

VEGAN CHOCOLATE CUPCAKES

There's no dairy in sight with these cupcakes, but they are still creamy and rich.

METHOD

Preheat the oven to 350°F and line a 12-cup muffin pan with liners. Mash the bananas in a large bowl. Then add the coconut oil, almond milk, vinegar, vanilla extract, and sugar, and mix thoroughly to combine.

Using a sieve, sift in the flour, baking powder, baking soda, cocoa powder, and salt. Stir well until everything is combined. Then fold in the chocolate chips.

Bake for 15 to 20 minutes, until a toothpick comes out clean, then transfer to a rack and let cool.

MAKES

10 to 12 cupcakes

INGREDIENTS

2 large, overripe bananas

2 tablespoons melted coconut oil

½ cup almond milk

1 teaspoon apple cider vinegar

1 teaspoon vanilla extract

¾ cup superfine sugar

2 cups all-purpose flour

1 teaspoon baking powder

¾ teaspoon baking soda

3 tablespoons cocoa powder

Pinch of salt

½ cup dairy-free chocolate chips

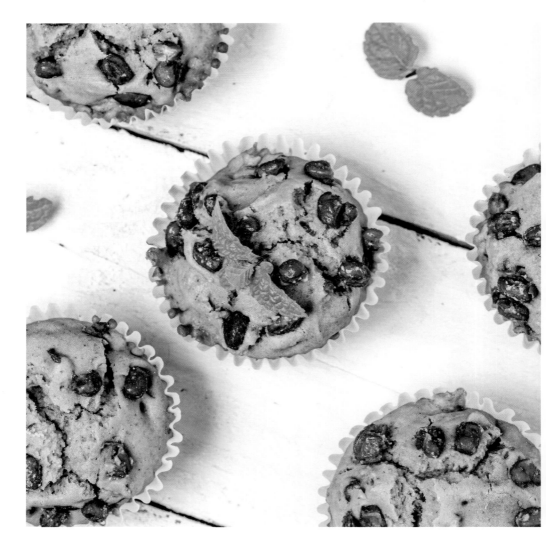

MATCHA AND BANANA CUPCAKES WITH CARAMELIZED PEANUTS

Packed with antioxidants and vitamins, matcha is truly one of the world's superfoods. Add it into these muffins, along with caramelized peanuts, for a healthy kick to a delicious treat.

METHOD

Preheat the oven to 350°F and line a 12-cup muffin pan with liners.

In a large bowl, mash the bananas with a fork until smooth. Add in both sugars, the egg, and melted butter, and whisk until combined.

Using a sieve, sift the flour, baking powder, baking soda, salt, and matcha powder into the bowl and stir with a wooden spoon to combine.

Fold in the caramelized peanuts, and mix until they are evenly distributed.

Divide the mixture between the muffin liners and bake for 15 minutes, or until a toothpick comes out clean.

Let cool before serving. Store in an airtight container for up to 1 week.

MAKES

10 cupcakes

INGREDIENTS

2 large, overripe bananas

1/3 cup superfine sugar

1/4 cup light brown sugar

1 egg

1/4 cup butter, melted

1¾ cups self-rising flour

½ teaspoon baking powder

1 teaspoon baking soda

½ teaspoon salt

1 tablespoon matcha powder

2½ ounces caramelized peanuts

OATY BANANA MUFFINS

Whether you're looking for a snack, breakfast, or dessert, these oaty banana muffins have you covered.

METHOD

Preheat the oven to 350°F and line a 12-cup muffin pan with liners.

In a large bowl, mash the bananas with a fork until smooth. Add in both sugars, the egg, melted butter, vanilla extract, and milk, and whisk until combined.

Using a sieve, sift the flour, baking powder, baking soda, and salt into the bowl, and stir with a wooden spoon until incorporated. Fold in the oats until combined.

Divide the mixture between the muffin liners and sprinkle a few oats over the top of each one. Bake for 15 minutes, or until a toothpick comes out clean.

Let cool before serving. Store in an airtight container for up to 1 week.

MAKES

10 muffins

INGREDIENTS

2 large, overripe bananas

¼ cup superfine sugar

¼ cup light brown sugar

1 egg

½ cup butter, melted

½ teaspoon vanilla extract

½ cup milk

1½ cups self-rising flour

½ teaspoon baking powder

1 teaspoon baking soda

½ teaspoon salt

1 cup quick-cooking oats, plus 2 tablespoons, for topping

BANANA BUTTERCREAM FROSTING

Bring banana to any cake or cupcake with this easy buttercream frosting. It is great on the vegan chocolate cupcakes (p. 41).

METHOD

Mash the banana by hand, or purée it in a food processor, with the aim of getting it as smooth as possible.

Transfer to a large bowl, add the lemon juice, and stir well. Then add the butter and beat this into the banana with an electric hand mixer.

Add the sugar 1 cup at a time, stirring it in a little by hand before mixing with the hand mixer. When the frosting is ready, it should be a spreadable consistency and hold its shape. If your frosting reaches this stage before you've added all the sugar, stop. If your frosting is too stiff, add lemon juice, a drop or two at a time, and mix until you reach the desired consistency.

Spread the frosting on cupcakes or a large cake, or keep refrigerated in an airtight container for up to 1 week.

MAKES

enough for 10 to 12 cupcakes

INGREDIENTS

1 medium, overripe banana

½ teaspoon lemon juice

⅓ cup non-dairy butter, room temperature

3½ cups confectioners' sugar

GOOEY CHOCOLATE BROWNIES

In this recipe, banana is the magic ingredient that allows the classic brownie to become dairy-free.

METHOD

Preheat the oven to 350°F and line an 8-inch square pan with parchment paper.

In a large bowl, mash the bananas until smooth. Add the sugars and combine with an electric hand mixer. Then add the almond milk and vegetable oil, and mix again.

Put the coffee granules in a cup and dissolve them with 1 tablespoon boiling water. Add to the banana mixture and whisk to combine.

Using a sieve, sift in the flour, cocoa powder, salt, and baking powder. Fold this into the mixture by hand until everything is incorporated.

Transfer mixture to the prepared pan and bake for 15 minutes, or until a toothpick comes out clean. Remove from the oven and let cool in the pan for a few minutes before transferring to a cooling rack. Cut into 9 or 16 squares, depending on how big you would like them to be.

Store in an airtight container for up to 2 weeks.

MAKES

12 to 16 brownies

INGREDIENTS

2 large, overripe bananas

½ cup superfine sugar

½ cup light brown sugar

⅓ cup almond milk

¼ cup vegetable oil

1 teaspoon instant coffee granules

1 tablespoon boiling water

2¼ cups self-rising flour

1 cup cocoa powder

1 teaspoon salt

1 teaspoon baking powder

SMOOTHIES AND SHAKES

- Chocolate and Banana Milkshake
- Apple and Cinnamon Shake
- Avocado and Banana Smoothie
- Super-Green Smoothie
- Granola-Topped Berry Smoothie
- Peanut Butter and Banana Milkshake
- Banana Oat Smoothie
- Banana Iced Coffee

CHOCOLATE AND BANANA MILKSHAKE

This smoothie is simple but indulgent—ideal for a weekend treat.

METHOD

Place the banana, chocolate-flavored milk, cocoa powder, and ice cubes into a blender, and blend to combine.

If you prefer your smoothie to be sweeter, add agave syrup, 1 teaspoon at a time, until you reach the desired sweetness.

Transfer to a tall glass and serve immediately, topped with chocolate shavings, if desired.

SERVES

1

INGREDIENTS

1 large, overripe banana

¾ cup chocolate-flavored soy/almond milk

1 tablespoon cocoa powder

3 ice cubes

Agave syrup, to taste

Non-dairy chocolate shavings, for garnish

APPLE AND CINNAMON SHAKE

A dash of cinnamon makes this smoothie the perfect autumn refreshment.

METHOD

Core and chop the apple into chunks (but keep the peel on) and slice the banana. If the dates are not already soft, soak them in lukewarm water for 30 minutes, then drain.

Place the chopped fruit in a blender along with the dates, vanilla, milk, apple juice, cinnamon, almonds, yogurt, and ice cubes.

Blend until completely smooth and transfer to a glass. If desired, garnish with cinnamon. Serve immediately.

SERVES

1

INGREDIENTS

1 large apple

1 large, overripe banana

3 soft pitted dates

½ teaspoon vanilla extract

⅔ cup non-dairy milk

¼ cup apple juice

1 teaspoon ground cinnamon, plus extra for garnish

2 tablespoons almonds

2 tablespoons non-dairy plain yogurt

3 ice cubes

AVOCADO AND BANANA SMOOTHIE

Packed with the goodness of avocado and banana, this smoothie will fill you to the brim with get-up-and-go!

METHOD

Slice the banana, then add to a blender, along with the avocado and other ingredients, and blend until smooth.

Transfer to a glass and serve immediately.

SERVES

1

INGREDIENTS

1 small, overripe banana

Flesh of 1 avocado

1 teaspoon lemon juice

1 teaspoon agave syrup

½ teaspoon vanilla extract

¾ cup almond milk

3 ice cubes

SUPER-GREEN SMOOTHIE

Get your greens with this superfood smoothie!

METHOD

Slice the bananas, then add to a blender along with all the other ingredients. Blend until smooth.

Transfer to two glasses and serve immediately, topped with extra chia seeds, if desired.

SERVES

2

INGREDIENTS

2 small, overripe bananas

1½ ounces spinach

Flesh of 1 avocado

2 teaspoons chia seeds, plus extra for garnish

Flesh of 2 kiwis

1⅔ cups almond milk

6 ice cubes

GRANOLA-TOPPED BERRY SMOOTHIE

Combine two delicious breakfast varieties into one with this granola-topped smoothie, and get the best of both worlds!

METHOD

To make the granola, preheat the oven to 275°F. Spread the oats out on a baking sheet lined with parchment paper and toast them in the oven for 10 minutes. Then remove and wait for them to cool to room temperature.

Melt the coconut oil in a saucepan over medium heat, then add the agave nectar and nutmeg, and mix. Add the oats to the coconut-oil mixture and stir until they are coated.

Place the oats back on the baking sheet and toast them in the oven for 3 minutes. Remove from the oven and let cool. The granola can be stored in an airtight container at room temperature for up to 3 weeks.

To make the smoothie, place the yogurt, strawberries, banana, raspberries, oat milk, and ice cubes into a blender and blend until smooth. Add more milk if the smoothie is too thick.

Pour into a glass and sprinkle a handful of granola on top of the smoothie. Add dried fruit for extra flavor, if desired. Serve immediately.

SERVES

1 (plus extra granola)

INGREDIENTS

For the granola:

½ cup rolled oats

1 teaspoon coconut oil

1 tablespoon agave nectar, plus extra to taste

Pinch of ground nutmeg

For the smoothie:

1 tablespoon non-dairy plain yogurt

¼ cup strawberries, hulled

1 medium, overripe banana

⅓ cup raspberries

⅔ cup oat milk

3 ice cubes

Dried fruit (optional)

PEANUT BUTTER AND BANANA MILKSHAKE

With its sweet, nutty flavor, this milkshake is sure to become a favorite.

METHOD

Place the banana, milk, peanut butter, and ice cubes into a blender, and blend to combine.

If you prefer your milkshake to be sweeter, add agave syrup, 1 teaspoon at a time, until you reach the desired sweetness.

Transfer to a glass and add a drizzle of peanut butter and a handful of chopped peanuts for garnish, if desired. Serve immediately.

SERVES

1

INGREDIENTS

1 large, overripe banana

¾ cup unsweetened almond milk

2 heaping tablespoons peanut butter

3 ice cubes

Agave syrup, to taste

Chopped peanuts, for garnish

Peanut butter, for garnish

BANANA OAT SMOOTHIE

This recipe transforms humble ingredients into a creamy and comforting smoothie.

METHOD

Place the banana, milk, oats, ice cubes, and pumpkin spice into a blender, and blend to combine.

If you prefer your smoothie to be sweeter, add agave syrup, 1 teaspoon at a time, until you reach the desired sweetness.

Transfer to a glass and top with a handful of lightly toasted oats for garnish, if desired. Serve immediately.

SERVES

1

INGREDIENTS

1 large, overripe banana
¾ cup oat milk
3 tablespoons rolled oats
3 ice cubes
½ teaspoon pumpkin spice
Agave syrup, to taste
Toasted oats, for garnish

BANANA ICED COFFEE

Give a caffeine kick to a traditional smoothie with this simple recipe.

METHOD

In a blender, combine all ingredients until smooth. Adjust the consistency to your liking by adding more milk or ice cubes.

Transfer to a glass and top with extra coffee beans and cinnamon, if desired. Serve immediately.

SERVES

1

INGREDIENTS

2 tablespoons espresso or strong coffee, cold

1 small, overripe banana

$\frac{1}{3}$ cup non-dairy milk

1 tablespoon maple syrup

$\frac{1}{4}$ teaspoon ground cinnamon, plus extra for garnish

3 ice cubes

Coffee beans, for garnish

SWEET TREATS

- Banana and Cinnamon Rolls
- Pumpkin and Sunflower Seed Cookies
- Pan-Fried Bananas with
  Salted Caramel Sauce
- Battered Bananas with Coconut
- Banana Bread
- Banana and Cherry Jam Crepes
- Banana and Chocolate Tart
- Banoffee Millionaire's Shortbread

BANANA AND CINNAMON ROLLS

There's not much you can do to improve on the classic cinnamon roll—except perhaps by adding banana!

METHOD

Line an 8-inch square tray with parchment paper. To make the filling, mash the banana until smooth, then mix it with the butter. In a separate bowl, add the cinnamon, cocoa powder, sugar, and salt. Stir briefly to mix.

Roll out the pastry on a floured surface to roughly form a 14 by 8-inch rectangle. Spread the banana mixture evenly over it, then add a layer of the cinnamon mixture. Top with the chocolate chips. Then roll up the pastry from the long side. Slice the pastry into nine equal parts, and place each one on the prepared tray with a swirl facing up. Cover the tray loosely with foil, and leave for 1 hour in a warm place to rise.

Preheat the oven to 325°F. Remove the foil and bake the rolls for 20 to 25 minutes, until they have started to turn golden. If they begin to brown too quickly, then replace the foil loosely over the tray.

While the rolls are baking, make the glaze by mixing the confectioners' sugar and vanilla extract together. Add the milk, a few drops at a time, until the glaze is smooth and thick. Cover with cling wrap and set aside.

When the rolls are done, let them cool on a rack. When they are cool enough to touch, top with the glaze and serve immediately, or store in an airtight container for up to 5 days.

INGREDIENTS

For the filling:
1 medium, overripe banana

2 tablespoons unsalted butter, at room temperature

1½ tablespoons ground cinnamon

½ teaspoon cocoa powder

¼ cup brown sugar

Pinch of salt

⅓ cup dark chocolate chips

For the pastry:
1 block/sheet puff pastry (approximately 9 ounces)

For the glaze:
1⅓ cups confectioners' sugar

1 teaspoon vanilla extract

1 to 2 teaspoons milk

PUMPKIN AND SUNFLOWER SEED COOKIES

Don't be fooled by their size—these little cookies are bursting with energy and goodness.

METHOD

If they're not already soft, soak the dates in lukewarm water for 30 minutes, then drain. Preheat the oven to 300°F and line an 8-inch square sheet with parchment paper.

Blend the pumpkin and sunflower seeds into small pieces in a food processor and set aside. In a small cup, add the chia seeds with 3 tablespoons of cold water. Stir briefly and let stand for a few minutes, or until the mixture has thickened.

Blend the banana, dates, and agave syrup together in a food processor. Transfer to a bowl, then add the seeds and remaining ingredients. Stir until combined. Take 1 teaspoon of dough and press it into a cookie shape with your hands. Place on the prepared baking sheet and repeat until all the dough has been used.

Bake for 20 minutes, or until the edges of the cookies are starting to turn golden. Let cool before serving. Store in an airtight container for up to 2 weeks.

MAKES

12 to 16 cookies

INGREDIENTS

6 soft pitted dates

1¾ ounces pumpkin seeds

1 ounce sunflower seeds

1 tablespoon ground chia seeds

3 tablespoons cold water

1 large, overripe banana

1 teaspoon agave syrup

¾ cup rolled oats

⅓ cup raisins

⅓ cup cranberries

PAN-FRIED BANANAS WITH SALTED CARAMEL SAUCE

SERVES

2

This luxurious salted caramel sauce is so creamy you won't believe it's dairy-free.

METHOD

To make the sauce, add the sugar to a pan and warm over medium heat for 2 minutes, stirring occasionally. Then add the coconut milk and bring to a boil, stirring constantly.

Turn the heat down and allow the mixture to simmer for 15 to 20 minutes. Stir occasionally. When the mixture is sticky and has thickened slightly, remove from heat and stir in the vanilla and salt. Let cool to room temperature before using.

For the bananas, melt the coconut oil in a frying pan over medium heat. Add the banana slices, and cook on each side for 2 minutes.

Transfer to a plate and serve immediately, topped with the salted caramel sauce.

INGREDIENTS

For the sauce:
$\frac{1}{3}$ cup light brown sugar

$\frac{1}{2}$ cup full-fat coconut milk

$\frac{1}{2}$ teaspoon vanilla extract

Pinch of salt (or more, to taste)

For the bananas:
2 teaspoons coconut oil

2 large, overripe bananas, sliced

BATTERED BANANAS WITH COCONUT

This treat can get messy in the making, but it's worth it for the tasty end result!

METHOD

Sift the flour, cornmeal and salt into a bowl, add the sugar, and mix together. In a separate bowl, combine the milk, eggs, and coconut extract. Add to the flour mixture and whisk until the batter is smooth.

Cut the bananas in half at the midpoint.

Pour the oil into a medium-sized pan with a lid and heat it very gradually over medium-low heat. Test the heat by dropping a tiny bit of batter in. If it sizzles immediately, it's ready.

Dip each piece of banana in the batter, then gently transfer it to the pan with tongs or two forks. Cook on each side for about 1 minute. Transfer the fried bananas to a paper towel to absorb excess oil, then move to a plate.

Dust with confectioners' sugar, and chocolate sauce if desired, and serve immediately.

INGREDIENTS

¾ cup all-purpose flour

3 tablespoons cornmeal

Pinch of salt

2 teaspoons superfine sugar

⅓ cup milk

2 eggs

4 drops coconut extract

4 medium, overripe bananas

1⅔ cups oil

2 tablespoons confectioners' sugar, for garnish

Chocolate sauce, for garnish

BANANA BREAD

Try this recipe for the American classic: banana bread.

METHOD

Preheat the oven to 350°F and line a 6 by 3½-inch loaf pan with parchment paper.

In a large bowl, cream the butter and sugars together until the mixture is light and fluffy. Then add the eggs, and beat well.

In a separate bowl, sift together the almond meal, flour, baking powder, and salt. Stir briefly to mix, then add into the egg mixture, and fold it in with a spatula. If the mixture is very stiff and difficult to stir, add 1 tablespoon of milk to loosen it.

Finally, add the mashed bananas into the batter, and stir until well distributed. Pour the mixture into the prepared loaf pan. Slice the remaining banana lengthwise down the middle. Place each piece flat side up on top of the batter.

Bake for 20 minutes, then cover the pan loosely with foil to prevent the top from burning and bake for 20 to 25 minutes more, until a toothpick comes out clean. Let cool for a few minutes in the pan before transferring to a rack to cool completely. Store in an airtight container for up to 1 week.

MAKES

1 loaf

INGREDIENTS

1⅓ cups butter, softened

⅓ cup superfine sugar

¼ cup soft brown sugar

2 eggs, room temperature

2 tablespoons almond meal

1½ cups self-rising flour

1 teaspoon baking powder

½ teaspoon salt

1 tablespoon milk

2 large, overripe bananas, mashed

1 medium, overripe banana, for decoration

BANANA AND CHERRY JAM CREPES

It doesn't have to be Pancake Day—these crepes make a great dessert all year' round.

METHOD

To make the batter, place the flour and salt into a large bowl and stir briefly to combine. In a separate bowl, whisk together the eggs and milk. Once combined, add to the flour and whisk until the batter is smooth.

Place a small amount of butter into a frying pan over medium heat. Once the butter has melted, spoon some of the batter into the pan and quickly spread it so the pan base is thinly coated. Cook for about 1 minute, until the bottom of the crepe is golden brown, then flip and cook the other side for another minute. Transfer onto a plate and set aside in a warm oven while you cook the other crepes.

To assemble, spread a thin layer of cherry jam on the crepes, add a few banana slices to each, and finish with a quick drizzle of lemon juice and some chocolate sprinkles. Then fold the crepes as desired and serve immediately.

MAKES

10 to 12 crepes

INGREDIENTS

For the crepes:
1¼ cups all-purpose flour
½ teaspoon salt
3 eggs
1½ cups milk
Pat of butter, for frying

For the filling:
Jar of cherry jam
4 large, overripe bananas, sliced
1 lemon, cut into small wedges
Chocolate sprinkles

BANANA AND CHOCOLATE TART

This fancy dessert is, in fact, very simple to make (but don't tell your friends!).

METHOD

To make the chocolate ganache filling, chop the chocolate into small pieces, transfer to a heatproof bowl, and set aside. Place the cream and sugar into a pan over medium heat, and stir gently until it's just below boiling point (it will be steaming, and tiny bubbles will appear around the edge of the pan). Pour the cream slowly over the chocolate, and leave it for 2 minutes. Then mix the ganache with a whisk or spatula until it becomes smooth and glossy. Add the butter and salt and keep whisking until the butter has melted.

Layer the bottom of each tartlet with the banana slices. Divide the ganache between the two tarts, filling each one to the brim. Refrigerate for at least 1 hour to set the ganache.

For the decorations, use a vegetable peeler to peel shavings off the white chocolate. When the ganache has set, sprinkle the white chocolate curls around the edge of each tart and top with banana chips, if desired.

INGREDIENTS

For the pastry:

2 medium
   pastry tartlets

For the filling:

6¼ ounces dark chocolate

⅔ cup heavy
   whipping cream

1 teaspoon superfine
   sugar

1½ tablespoons butter,
   in small chunks

Pinch of salt

1 medium, overripe
   banana, sliced

For the decorations:

White chocolate, room
   temperature

Dried banana chips
   (p. 35), for garnish

BANOFFEE MILLIONAIRE'S SHORTBREAD

Make your friends and family feel like a million dollars with this luxurious treat.

METHOD

Line an 8-inch square pan with parchment paper. To make the shortbread, in a large bowl cream the butter and sugar together until light and fluffy. Sift in the flour and salt, and stir until you have a smooth dough. Press the dough into the bottom of the baking pan, prick the top lightly with a fork, and refrigerate for 1 hour.

Preheat the oven to 350°F and bake the shortbread for 15 to 20 minutes, until the top begins to turn golden. Leave in the pan to cool. To make the banana caramel, purée the banana in a food processor, then strain it to remove any lumps, helping the mixture through with the back of a spoon. Combine the coconut milk, sugars, and vanilla in a pan, slowly bring to a boil, and keep it bubbling over medium heat for a few minutes, stirring continuously until the caramel thickens. Then stir in the banana, and let cool for a few minutes. Spread the caramel over the shortbread and refrigerate for 1 hour, or until set.

Melt the dark chocolate in a bowl over a pan of simmering water. Stir occasionally. Once melted, spread over the top of the set caramel layer. Use a knife or spatula to make it smooth. Refrigerate until set, then remove from the pan, slice, and serve. Store in an airtight container for up to 1 week.

MAKES
10 to 12 squares

INGREDIENTS

For the shortbread:
1½ cups non-dairy butter
⅓ cup superfine sugar
1¾ cups all-purpose flour
Pinch of salt

For the caramel:
1 small, overripe banana
¾ cup full-fat coconut milk
¼ cup light brown sugar
2 tablespoons superfine sugar
½ teaspoon vanilla extract

For the topping:
12⅓ ounces non-dairy dark chocolate, chopped

FROZEN SWEETS

- Miracle Banana Ice Cream
- Banana, Cashew, and Chocolate Ice Cream
- Mint Chocolate Chip Banana Ice Cream
- Summer Strawberry and Banana Sorbet
- Chocolate Fudge Popsicles
- Banana Popsicles
- Cherry and Banana Ice Cream Sandwiches

MIRACLE BANANA ICE CREAM

SERVES

4

INGREDIENTS

4 large, overripe
   bananas

You'll be hard-pressed to find a recipe simpler than this one-ingredient wonder!

METHOD

Peel and roughly slice the bananas, and place in an airtight, freezer-safe container. Freeze the bananas for at least 3 hours, or overnight, or until they are completely frozen.

To make the ice cream, begin by pulsing the frozen bananas in a food processor. As they begin to break up, blend continuously until the mixture becomes smooth and thick. You may have to stop and scrape down the sides every now and then.

Once the mixture is smooth, return it to the freezer-safe container and freeze again for a short time until it has set. Then, serve!

This simple recipe can be spiced up any way you want. After the banana has been blended, try mixing in spices such as nutmeg and cinnamon, a handful of your favorite berries, or some nuts, such as pistachios or walnuts.

BANANA, CASHEW, AND CHOCOLATE ICE CREAM

Chocolate, banana, and creamy cashews make this ice cream a winner.

METHOD

Roughly slice the bananas, and place in an airtight, freezer-safe container. Freeze the bananas for at least 3 hours, or overnight, or until they are completely frozen.

While the bananas are freezing, soak the cashews in water (ideally overnight).

To make the ice cream, begin by pulsing the frozen bananas in a food processor. As they begin to break up, blend continuously until the mixture becomes smooth and thick. You may have to stop and scrape down the sides every now and then.

When the mixture is smooth, drain and add the cashews and cocoa powder. Blend for a further minute until combined.

Return the ice cream to the freezer to set. Serve topped with the walnuts, if desired.

SERVES

4

INGREDIENTS

4 large, overripe bananas

⅔ cup cashews

4 tablespoons cocoa powder

Handful of walnuts, broken into pieces, for garnish

MINT CHOCOLATE CHIP BANANA ICE CREAM

Try this classic flavor with a twist!

METHOD

Peel and roughly slice the bananas, and place in an airtight, freezer-safe container. Freeze the bananas for at least 3 hours, or overnight, until they are completely frozen.

To make the ice cream, begin by pulsing the frozen bananas in a food processor. As they start to break up, blend continuously until the mixture becomes smooth and thick. You may have to stop and scrape down the sides every now and then.

When the mixture is smooth, add the peppermint extract and chocolate chips. Blend for 1 minute more until combined.

Return the ice cream to the freezer in the airtight, freezer-safe container to set. Serve topped with extra chocolate chips, if desired.

SERVES

4

INGREDIENTS

4 large, overripe bananas

2 teaspoons peppermint extract

¾ cup dairy-free chocolate chips, plus extra for garnish

SUMMER STRAWBERRY AND BANANA SORBET

Be transported to summertime with this fresh and fruity sorbet.

METHOD

Peel and roughly slice the bananas, wash and hull the strawberries, and place the fruit in an airtight, freezer-safe container. Freeze for at least 3 hours, or overnight, until they are completely frozen.

To make the ice cream, begin by pulsing the frozen fruit in a food processor. As it begins to break up, blend continuously until it becomes smooth and thick. You may have to stop and scrape down the sides every now and then.

When the mixture is smooth, return it to the freezer in the airtight, freezer-safe container to set. Serve topped with extra strawberries, if desired.

SERVES

4

INGREDIENTS

4 large, overripe bananas

$2\frac{1}{3}$ cups strawberries, plus extra for garnish

CHOCOLATE FUDGE POPSICLES

This frozen dessert is a great treat for hot summer days.

METHOD

Preheat the oven to 350°F and roast the hazelnuts for 5 minutes. Remove the skins, then blend them in a food processor along with the vegetable oil until they turn into a paste. This should take a few minutes.

Meanwhile, put the dates in a pan with ½ cup of water and simmer for 5 minutes, or until nearly all the liquid is gone.

Add the bananas, cocoa powder, dates (plus any remaining liquid), and coconut milk to the food processor with the hazelnut paste, and blend until smooth.

Distribute the mixture equally between the popsicle molds, add the popsicle stick/lid, and freeze overnight.

To remove the popsicles from the molds, place them in warm water until you can pull the popsicle away from the mold.

Eat immediately, or store them frozen in an airtight container for up to 1 month.

MAKES

8 popsicles

INGREDIENTS

½ cup hazelnuts

1 teaspoon vegetable oil

3 ounces soft pitted dates, chopped

½ cup water

2 large, overripe bananas

2 tablespoons cocoa powder

1 cup full-fat coconut milk

EXTRA EQUIPMENT

8 popsicle molds and 8 popsicle sticks (or a reusable popsicle mold set)

BANANA POPSICLES

These treats are the banana's answer to the caramel apple.

METHOD

Preheat the oven to 250°F and line two large baking sheets with parchment paper. To make the meringue, place the aquafaba and lemon juice in a bowl, and mix with an electric hand mixer until white, glossy peaks begin to form. This should take a few minutes. Then add the sugar in gradually, mixing constantly. Continue to whip until the meringue holds stiff peaks. If you would like, add a drop of food coloring to the meringue at this point.

Transfer the meringue to a piping bag, snip off the end, and pipe small rounds onto one of the prepared trays. Bake for 45 minutes, then turn the oven off and leave the meringues inside for another hour to dry out. Once done, remove from the oven and let cool. Then break them into different-sized pieces.

To make the popsicles, chop the bananas in half. Melt the chocolate in a bowl over a saucepan of simmering water. Toothpick the banana halves onto sticks and dip them in the chocolate. Decorate with the crushed meringue pieces while the chocolate is still melted, and leave on the other large tray to set. Freeze for at least 30 minutes, then serve. Store them frozen in an airtight container for up to 1 month.

MAKES

5 popsicles

INGREDIENTS

For the meringue:
½ cup aquafaba (water from can of chickpeas)

¼ teaspoon lemon juice

½ cup superfine sugar

Food coloring (optional)

For the popsicles:
5 medium, overripe bananas

7 ounces non-dairy milk chocolate

EXTRA EQUIPMENT

5 popsicle sticks

CHERRY AND BANANA ICE CREAM SANDWICHES

What's better than ice cream? Cookies *and* ice cream! We've suggested using cherries, but this recipe works well with any summer fruit.

METHOD

Roughly slice the bananas, and place in an airtight, freezer-safe container. Freeze the bananas for at least 3 hours, or overnight, until they are completely frozen.

To make the ice cream, begin by pulsing the frozen bananas in a food processor. As they begin to break up, blend continuously until the mixture becomes smooth and thick. You may have to stop and scrape down the sides every now and then.

Once the mixture is smooth, add in the cherries and pulse until they are just beginning to break up. Return the mixture to the freezer-safe container and freeze for a short time until it sets again. Serve the ice cream sandwiched between two cookies.

If you want to take this recipe to the next level, why not try it with the cookies on p. 73?

MAKES

4 ice cream sandwiches

INGREDIENTS

2 large, overripe bananas

$1^2/_3$ cups cherries, pitted

8 chocolate chip cookies

DELICIOUS
DESSERTS

- Banoffee Pie
- Banana Upside-Down Cake
- Frosted Banana Cake
- Apple and Banana Crumble
- No-Bake Peanut Butter Cheesecake
- Creamy Custard Tarts
- Raw Chocolate and Walnut Tart
- No-Bake Banana Cheesecake
- Banana, Maple, and Hazelnut Semolina Pudding
- No-Bake Strawberry and Banana Mini Cheesecakes

BANOFFEE PIE

Is there any other desert quite as distinctive as banoffee pie? Probably not! Here's a simple recipe for this classic 1970s dessert.

METHOD

Grease an 8-inch round springform pan.

Blend all the cookies in a food processor—or crush them with a rolling pin—then add the melted butter and mix again until the cookies are coated. Pack the crumbs into the bottom of your pan and refrigerate for 1 hour.

Spread the caramel over the cookie base, then add a layer of bananas on top.

In a medium bowl, whisk the cream until it is thick and light. Spread or pipe over the bananas, then grate the chocolate over the top. Keep refrigerated and consume within 3 days.

SERVES

10 to 12

INGREDIENTS

For the crust:
Pat of butter, for greasing
40 graham crackers,
    or 10 sheets
14 ginger snaps
1 cup butter, melted

For the caramel:
1 jar caramel topping
    (approximately
    14 ounces)

For the topping:
3 medium, overripe
    bananas, sliced
¾ cup heavy
    whipping cream
1¾ ounces chocolate
    of choice

BANANA UPSIDE-DOWN CAKE

Try this twist on the traditional upside-down cake, featuring bananas and a spicy-sweet hint of cardamom.

METHOD

Preheat the oven to 350°F and line an 8-inch square pan with parchment paper.

To make the topping, in a medium bowl beat the butter and sugar until light and fluffy. Add the cardamom and salt, and beat again until mixed. Spread over the bottom of the pan, then arrange the banana halves, flat side down, over the mixture.

Place the butter, flour, sugars, salt, cardamom, cinnamon, and baking powder in a large bowl, and mix with an electric hand mixer until combined. Add the eggs and vanilla extract, and beat well. Layer the mixture on top of the bananas and bake for 25 to 30 minutes, until a toothpick comes out clean. Let the cake cool for 30 minutes before turning it out onto a rack. Keep in an airtight container and consume within 1 week.

INGREDIENTS

For the topping:

½ cup butter

¼ cup packed light brown sugar

½ teaspoon cardamom

Pinch of salt

9 to 10 small, overripe bananas, halved lengthwise

For the cake:

1⅓ cups butter, softened

1¼ cups self-rising flour

½ cup superfine sugar

¼ cup light brown sugar

Pinch of salt

½ teaspoon cardamom

½ teaspoon ground cinnamon

½ teaspoon baking powder

2 eggs

½ teaspoon vanilla extract

FROSTED BANANA CAKE

This is the perfect coffee-break cake—best enjoyed while you have your feet up!

METHOD

Preheat the oven to 350°F and grease two 8-inch round cake pans.

In a large bowl, cream the sugar and butter together. Add the banana and beat until incorporated. Sift in the flour, baking powder, baking soda, and salt, and fold in. Then stir in the hazelnuts and vinegar.

Divide the mixture between the two pans and bake for 15 minutes, or until a toothpick comes out clean. Place on a rack to cool.

To make the frosting, beat the butter, sugar, and vanilla extract together in a large bowl. If the frosting is too stiff to spread, add milk, a few drops at a time, to soften it.

Sandwich the two cakes together with frosting, then cover the cake with the remaining frosting. Decorate with banana chips, if desired. Keep in an airtight container and consume within 1 week.

SERVES

10 to 12

INGREDIENTS

For the cake:
¾ cup superfine sugar
½ cup non-dairy butter, plus extra for greasing
3 large, overripe bananas, mashed
2¼ cups self-rising flour
1 teaspoon baking powder
1 teaspoon baking soda
Pinch of salt
⅓ cup hazelnuts, chopped
1 tablespoon apple cider vinegar

For the icing:
1½ cups non-dairy butter
2⅔ cups confectioners' sugar
½ teaspoon vanilla extract
2 tablespoons non-dairy milk
Banana chips (p. 35), for garnish

APPLE AND BANANA CRUMBLE

This crumble recipe is easily made dairy and gluten-free—something that everybody can enjoy.

METHOD

Preheat the oven to 350°F and grease an 8-inch ovenproof dish.

To make the filling, place the fruit into a large saucepan along with 1 tablespoon of water and 1 tablespoon of the sugar. Cook the fruit uncovered on low heat for 5 minutes, stirring occasionally, or until it has softened a little. Then add the rest of the sugar, flour, cinnamon, and salt. Stir thoroughly to combine and set aside.

Meanwhile, put all the topping ingredients into a bowl and blend together using a pastry cutter or fork until it resembles breadcrumbs.

Put the fruit mixture into the bottom of the prepared dish, then sprinkle the crumble topping over the fruit evenly.

Bake for 30 to 40 minutes, until the fruit is bubbling and the top is golden brown. Let cool on a cooling rack before serving. Keep refrigerated and consume within 3 days.

SERVES
8 to 10

INGREDIENTS

For the filling:
Pat of non-dairy butter, for greasing

2½ cups cooking apples, peeled and chopped

1 medium banana, lightly mashed

¼ cup light brown sugar

1 tablespoon all-purpose flour (or gluten-free flour)

1 teaspoon cinnamon

½ teaspoon salt

For the topping:
1⅔ cups all-purpose flour (or gluten-free flour)

2 tablespoons light brown sugar

1⅓ cups non-dairy butter

Pinch of salt

NO-BAKE PEANUT BUTTER CHEESECAKE

There's no cooking required for this rich, nutty cheesecake.

METHOD

Grease an 8-inch round springform pan.

Blend the cookies in a food processor until they are crumbs. Melt the butter, then add to the cookies, and mix again until combined. Press the crust mixture into the pan and refrigerate for 1 hour.

Purée the bananas in a food processor and strain through a sieve to get rid of any lumps, pushing it through with the back of a spoon if needed. Then add the puree back to the food processor along with the cashews (drained), coconut oil, milk, water, lemon juice, and peanut butter. Blend until smooth. Spread the mixture over the biscuit crust and refrigerate for another 2 hours.

Before serving, chop the chocolate into small pieces and melt it in a bowl over a saucepan of simmering water. Drizzle over the cheesecake and add a sprinkling of peanuts. Keep refrigerated and consume within 3 days.

SERVES

8 to 10

INGREDIENTS

For the crust:

1 cup non-dairy butter,
    plus extra for greasing
9 ounces non-dairy oat cookies

For the filling:

2 medium, overripe bananas
1⅔ cups cashews, soaked
    overnight in water
½ cup coconut oil
⅓ cup non-dairy milk
1 tablespoon water
Juice of 1 lemon
2 tablespoons peanut butter

For the topping:

3½ ounces dark chocolate
Peanuts

CREAMY CUSTARD TARTS

These little tarts are almost too pretty to eat! (Almost . . .)

METHOD

Preheat the oven to 350°F and grease and line four 4-inch tart pans. Divide the pastry into four. Roll out one piece to at least a 5-inch circle, press it into the tart pan, and cut off the excess. Prick the bottom lightly with a fork. Repeat for the other three pieces.

Cover the top of the pastry pans with parchment paper and weigh each one down with pie weights or uncooked rice. Bake for 10 minutes. Then remove the paper and weights, and bake for 10 to 15 minutes more, until the pastry is golden. Remove and let cool on a rack. Put one of the bananas in a food processor and blend until smooth, then strain it to remove any lumps, pushing the mixture through with the back of a spoon if needed. Set to one side.

Heat the custard in a small pan, then add the banana puree and banana extract, and stir until incorporated. Heat until the custard is steaming. Divide the custard between each tart pan, let cool for a few minutes, and then refrigerate for 1 hour. Once the custard is completely cool, slice the second banana and top the tarts with the banana and strawberry slices and a few mint leaves, if desired. Keep refrigerated and consume within 3 days.

MAKES

4 tarts

INGREDIENTS

For the pastry:

Pat of butter, for greasing

8½ ounces sweet shortcrust pastry

For the filling:

2 large, overripe bananas

2 cups vanilla custard

½ teaspoon banana extract

1⅓ cups strawberries, sliced

Mint leaves, for garnish

RAW CHOCOLATE AND WALNUT TART

This smooth and creamy tart is the perfect dessert to round off your meal.

METHOD

If they're not already soft, soak the dates in lukewarm water for 30 minutes, then drain (the dates for the crust and filling can be soaked and drained at the same time).

Grease an 8-inch round springform pan. To make the crust, blend the almond meal, coconut, almond butter, coconut oil, and 4 dates in a food processor until a dough has formed. Press the dough into the pan so it covers the whole surface, and refrigerate for 1 hour.

For the filling, blend the remaining dates, banana, coconut oil, salt, and cocoa powder until smooth. Stir in the chopped walnuts and spread over the crust. Freeze for 3 hours.

For the topping, melt the chocolate in a bowl over a saucepan of simmering water. Add the melted coconut oil, and stir until combined. Spread the chocolate thinly over the tart while it's still frozen, then refrigerate until the chocolate has set. Bring to room temperature to serve. Keep refrigerated and consume within 3 days.

SERVES

8 to 10

INGREDIENTS

For the filling:
5¼ ounces soft pitted dates
1 small, overripe banana
4 tablespoons coconut oil, melted
Pinch of salt
½ tablespoon cocoa powder
⅔ cup walnuts, chopped

For the crust:
Pat of non-dairy butter,
    for greasing
3 cups almond meal
1⅓ cups shredded coconut
4 tablespoons almond butter
4 tablespoons coconut oil, melted
4 soft pitted dates

For the topping:
5¼ ounces non-dairy dark chocolate
1 teaspoon coconut oil, melted

NO-BAKE BANANA CHEESECAKE

This classic recipe is beautiful on its own, but can be customized with your favorite fruits and sauces.

METHOD

Grease an 8-inch round springform pan.

Blend the cookies in a food processor until they are crumbs. Melt the butter, then add to the cookies, and mix again until combined. Press the crust mixture into the bottom and sides of the pan, and refrigerate for 1 hour.

Purée the bananas in a food processor and strain through a sieve to get rid of any lumps, pressing it through with the back of a spoon if needed. Then add the puree back to the food processor along with the cashews (drained), sugar, coconut oil, milk, almond butter, banana extract, water, and lemon juice. Blend until smooth. Spread the mixture over the biscuit crust and refrigerate for another 2 hours.

Top with your favorite fruit, and serve with caramel sauce if desired. Keep refrigerated and consume within 3 days.

SERVES

8 to 10

INGREDIENTS

For the crust:

9 ounces non-dairy oat cookies

1 cup non-dairy butter, plus extra for greasing

For the filling:

2 medium, overripe bananas

$1\frac{1}{3}$ cups cashews, soaked overnight in water

$\frac{1}{4}$ cup confectioners' sugar

$\frac{1}{4}$ cup coconut oil

$\frac{1}{3}$ cup non-dairy milk

1 tablespoon almond butter

1 teaspoon banana extract

1 tablespoon water

Juice of 1 lemon

Fruit

Caramel sauce

BANANA, MAPLE, AND HAZELNUT SEMOLINA PUDDING

This winter warmer is comforting and filling—just the thing for cozy nights in.

METHOD

Put the milk, semolina, sugar, and salt in a saucepan over medium heat. Stir continuously until the mixture begins to thicken. This should take a few minutes.

Once it's thick, simmer the semolina mixture for 2 minutes, stirring continuously. Then remove from the heat and stir in the nut butter.

Divide the mixture between four bowls, and top with banana slices, hazelnuts, and maple syrup. Serve immediately.

SERVES

4

INGREDIENTS

2 cups non-dairy milk

¼ cup fine semolina

2 teaspoons light brown sugar

Pinch of salt

1 tablespoon hazelnut butter (or other nut butter)

1 medium, overripe banana, sliced

⅓ cup hazelnuts, roughly chopped

4 tablespoons maple syrup

NO-BAKE STRAWBERRY AND BANANA MINI CHEESECAKES

These beautiful mini cheesecakes pack a fruity flavor punch!

METHOD

Grease a 12-cup muffin pan. Cut out 24 thin strips of parchment paper, each one approximately 6 inches long and ½ inch wide. Take two strips of paper per muffin cup, and place them in a cross shape in the well. The tabs should stick up over the top of the tray and will enable you to pull the cheesecakes out easily when they're set.

Blend the cookies in a food processor until they are crumbs. Melt the butter, then add to the cookies, and mix again until combined. Divide the crust mixture into 12 and press one portion into each cup in the pan. Refrigerate for 1 hour.

Purée the banana in a food processor and strain through a sieve to get rid of any lumps, using the back of a spoon to push it through. Set aside. Do the same for the strawberries. Add the cashews (drained), coconut oil, milk, almond butter, water, and lemon juice to a food processor and blend until smooth. Divide the mixture into two. Stir the banana puree into one and the strawberry puree into the other.

Spread the banana mixture over the crusts, filling the wells to about two-thirds full. Refrigerate for 30 minutes. Then fill the wells the rest of the way with the strawberry mixture. Refrigerate for 2 hours.

Serve topped with extra strawberries and a sprig of mint, if desired. Keep refrigerated and consume within 3 days.

MAKES
12 mini cheesecakes

INGREDIENTS

For the crust:

9 ounces non-dairy oat cookies

1 cup non-dairy butter, plus extra for greasing

For the filling:

1 medium, overripe banana

⅔ cup strawberries, plus extra for serving

1½ cups cashews, soaked overnight in water

¼ cup coconut oil

⅓ cup non-dairy milk

1 tablespoon almond butter

1 tablespoon water

Juice of 1 lemon

Mint leaves, for garnish

RECIPE INDEX

IMAGE CREDITS